INTERFERENCE
WITH THE Hydrangea

INTERFERENCE
WITH THE Hydrangea

MARI-LOU ROWLEY

thistledown press

National Library of Canada Cataloguing in Publication Data

Rowley, Mari-Lou, 1953-
Interference with the hydrangea / Mari-Lou Rowley.

Poems.
ISBN 1-894345-55-X

I. Title.
PS8585.O8957I57 2003   C811'.54   C2003-911115-6

Cover painting, *Cradle*, by Betsy Rosenwald
Book and cover design by J. Forrie
Typeset by Thistledown Press

Thistledown Press Ltd.
633 Main Street
Saskatoon, Saskatchewan, S7H 0J8
www.thistledown.sk.ca

Thistledown Press gratefully acknowledges the financial assistance of
the Canada Council for the Arts, the Saskatchewan Arts Board, and
the Government of Canada through the Book Publishing Industry
Development Program for its publishing program.

For Robert McNealy

CONTENTS

I CONFESSIONS

II REL(EV)ATIONS

CONFESSIONS

1st Confession

You love but without disturbance, are jealous but without care.
— St. Augustine

Daffodil sun and running
along still snowy ridges
swells of crocuses so blue the light
glissades with the wind
winding fingers through hair
jealous without care
it nudges, pushes
go, go   grow
away.

Today an owl sweeps a vector across snow
tiny birds eat from the altar of your hand
stand still as the virgin, feel the prick
of their claws, tenuous, delicate
a forbidden kiss.

Love without disturbance
in the sanctity of your touch
the thrill of running
so high so light   outside
the moon, melting snow, night
inside, the bed
soft as crocuses.

> *"The house of my soul is narrow for your entry."*
> — St. Augustine

Insignificant birds perched on mizzen
hitching a ride to sea
their thin songs muffled by flapping rags
of the lowest tattered sail
waiting for wind.

Somewhere in an alley they squat with needles
shooting for calm amidst fury
rain pools with blood and urine
they wait for sun as the fix fades.

The house of my soul is narrow for your entry
doorway thin as a mitre's crack
step through sideways
onto the cracked, parched earth
sit, and wait for rain.

3RD CONFESSION

> *"Birdlime compounded with syllables of your name . . . "*
> — St. Augustine

rapture trapped and ruptured
in public, an event almost
   this disentrailing,
snared remnants of skin
atrial shudder
   the heart's fissure.

birdlime compounded with syllables
   of your name
spoken haltingly, phonemes
stuck to incisors
biting bearing downturn
   of lips to gravity
teeth embedded in lost history
usurped, home again
   but not,
inhaling handful after handful
of all this wind.

> *"Do not let my soul be bound to words*
> *by the glue of love through the body's senses."*
> — St. Augustine

this chair, window, tree
data transmuted into the moment
of a poem, dative
the pairing of sense to soul
bound by words, a process
sticky as the *glue of love*

unbridled beneath a dome of stars
Orion's broad shoulders, jewelled sword
brilliant, potent in Artemis' absence

chastity pins virility to
the wall of night
beguiling in her tucked-up gown
moon goddess rails fury in a quiver
of arrows, blows monsoons
through the body's senses.

5TH CONFESSION

> *What in that theft delighted me . . .*
> *not even that false and shadowy beauty*
> *which belongs to deceiving vices.*
>
> — St. Augustine

A dream of stealing
motorcycles for the love of
speed and quick escapes.
What in that theft delighted me?

Forbidden fruit
sweet on the tongue?
The complicity of wind,
a sirocco's laugh
licking the place
taut with fields of energy,
the promise of freedom
somewhere outside oneself.

Faster, faster its whisper drips
with *deceiving vices.*
Open your mouth wide,
let demons take flight.

Times lose no time; nor do they roll idly by;
through our senses they work strange
operations of the mind.

— St. Augustine

How to take what nature gives us.
Snow on a May day, an earful of wind,
a lisp, a limp, a heart full of rust.
Time rolls idly by. One cosmology
is to another — dust

particles awhirl in fickle winds
yesterday it was monads
looking for mirrors, others
with which to share discharges
of thought.

Now electrons pair,
share orbitals, break the law
that like repels like. Neutrinos
shift flavours on their journey
from the sun.

What do these *strange operations* reveal
but yearnings of the mind,
when everywhere glamorous smiles
stretched to sneers, arthritic hands
studded with African diamonds.

7TH CONFESSION

And I resolved in Thy sight, not tumultuously to tear,
but gently to withdraw, the service of my tongue
from the marts of lip-labour . . .

— St. Augustine

A word spun off
a sound spun
off a thought.

How to speak
discandied in your sight
to a dunnock,
its small dull chirp.
I want to roar and tear, put an end
to this tumult.

Desire, too, spun off thought.
Prie dieu, a kneeling desk for prayer
now the *mart of lip-labour,*
how to *gently withdraw*
the service of my tongue.

> *Which thing I was sighing for, bound as I was,*
> *not with another's irons, but my own iron will.*
> — St. Augustine

On flat bed of slate
under a soaring fir
groaning in the wind:
    I know what you are sighing for
    you minions, adored daughters,
    courtesans bound with tender irons
    gaolers to each other's ghosts.

The stone now cold against her back
a ganglion of nerves knot in her throat,
breastbone wrests a sigh
fragile as a wish, heavy as prayer:
    Not my own, my will, not iron
    another's.

9TH CONFESSION

> *For we have not yet utterly forgotten that,*
> *which we remember ourselves to have forgotten.*
> — St. Augustine

russet, your neck
after days on the mountain
the smell of earth, sun
on your skin
not utterly forgotten.
a dowling pinning my heart
so neatly down

remembering ourselves.
meals of rusks and apples
bed of fragrant sage
the frenzied haze of night
wolves and owls answering
our cries.

to have forgotten this is
to have forgotten everything.
scaped the silver off every mirror
burned every word
the ash settling in our throats
stifling even the saddest song.

For there is yet a little light in men; let them walk
let them walk, that the darkness overtake them not.
— St. Augustine

Look up. A stained sky, too much
of the wrong kind of light.
Mechanisms for destruction
form a macula on the Virgin's skin.

Let them walk
on layers of broken stone
the heart's sticky macadam,
clothed in jaconets, waterproof,
despair retractable as the claws
of cats, leaving no marks
but paw pads in their tracks.

Let them walk with the lope
of an innocent youth, the gleam
still fresh in his eye.
No dragline to his step,
just a dewclaw of darkness
that overtakes him not.

REL(EV)ATIONS

DREAMING MACHU PICCHU

Radiant energy: the only form of energy
that can exist in the absence of matter

It begins as always, shoeless and
miles and miles of pale yellow desert
the gritty caress of warm sand
each step billowing a cloud
of powdered clay and calcite
on and on
as the sun burnishes
skin copper, hair golden
artifacts gleaming
as the late afternoon shadow
points out and back
to mountains, a path
under a canopy of jungle
up and up, heady
expectation of bliss
this sanctuary of granite
its intricate geometry of interlocking rock
so precise not even moss, a drop
of sacrificial blood from llama
grazing the mesa meadow
can seep between the tight stones
no mortar to bind them, iron tools
to shape them, no wheel or animals
to carry them to this place
she returns to again and again

for a glimpse of his dark eyes sleepless
with the weight of history on his
wide shoulders she dreams to hold
bathe him in her warm pool, bask
in his radiant energy.

SURGERY IN C MINOR
For Charlie Kerr

Tomorrow he will take a pinprick
    of light   of sound
scan the rubbery atrial tissue
for the one point
where when pressed
stars go nova.

He will try to burn it
into brightness
this heart that quickens
too early, keeps pace with
hummingbirds and the clacking
of foreign consonants.
Try to slow it to the sound of vowels,
the air over an owl's wing.

Not perfect, I say. More like Gould's hum
between bars, slightly out
of key but oh so da de dum
the glow of sun on the residue of day
scattered cumulus in soft focus,
mountains blueing in the distance.

The touch of his long pale
fingers on ivory, pressing
notes like words and watching them
form into frosty suspended breath as he walks
along a frozen lakeshore of childhood.

I think of all those notes pressed with such pleasure
like grapes under the feet of buxom Italian
women heady with romance.

Gutenberg's press was really for wine
until he discovered words, like grapes
could be pressed. Language
was always something first heard
but now all those words lined up
and ordered into thoughts we read
before we hear their music.

All this while the sun disappears
the clouds turn deep violet,
I accept the sedative, hope
he understands a certain syncopation
is needed to feel words
like grapes or hearts bursting.

LEOPARD FROG

For Loren Teed

> *Toad-licker, the headlines say.*
> *Gary Murphy, dead at 32, the headstones says.*

Mottled green dorsolateral folds
the perfect camouflage
its body a piece of bark   a cluster
of tiny stones
what I see is a twinkle of light
a smirk in the dark   its eyes.

As I move, it hops
zigzags toward the water
I scoop it out
feel its tiny toes clawing
my cupped hand   a cell.

Imagine eyes   closed
to sight.
What he felt, tips of fingers
sensors probing each surface
the cool reptilian skin   a memory
of sand against face. Imagine
him putting it to his cheek,
tiny legs frog-kicking against
his hard palm, rapid
beating of its cold-blooded
heart.

He rotates his head
puts the squirming toad to his lips
sucks the bitter secretions   and waits
        for its spirit to possess him

flail his arms kick his legs out sideways
quicken his pulse
two rhythms melding
amphibian/mammal
warm blood/cold blood
fast/faster

until he feels what the toad feels
sees what it sees
eyes bugged out with the pressure of blood
pumped too fast
red and yellow streaks of light
slanting in   the dull pupil dilates
to take it all, a writhing jungle of
green/gold/black
as he roars a leopard's roar.

They take him away,
lock him in a warm cell
come back and find him
          hanging   like bait,
a toad on a string.

I wonder how the cane toad felt
captured for its heady nectar.
Was it freed to the grass and water,
did it ever recover? Or did it remain
stiff and terrified as the leopard frog
I returned to the sand.
Once the most widely scattered amphibian
in North America, now mysteriously
disappearing.

back
  to ground
face
  to sky
watching wrens
hunched wing to wing
          on the wire
a row of counters on a
celestial abacus

tiny buds of birds
    budding in
budding up against
  peep   peeping
above the din
          voices
not yet lost
in the cacophony of city
    floating up
          to wisps of cirrus
flimsy impressions
of hand-tied hay bales
elongated
mushroom clouds

RIVER POEM
For Robert

Remember the bridge, the edge, the drop
the thin cord of black water
       undulating   silent
as it slid between thighs of ice
a slow moving whisper
its struggle to stay liquid
its soft mantra
      it doesn't matter
      it doesn't matter
      it doesn't
               matter

pleading like a lover
for the weight of my body
just a step, a quick fall
and the river opens.

astride you I think of this
ride the waves welling up
in the black of your eye, open
to take you deep, deeper
ride and crest
immersed, surfacing

I smell your dark animal fear
recognize the terror
of submersion.

Venus di Milo

They say the farmer who found her
broke off her arms, buried them
under the silver sage, fragrant bay trees
browning in the Aegean sun
if only to say — she is ours,
sprung from the seeds of history
her arms once open
in invitation, embrace.

Now amphitheatres in ruin
who can understand a hero's quest,
lover's yearning, mother's revenge
without feeling the curve of her
cool marble palm against cheek.

lazy arch and plane of sandstone
  white flaking epidermis
  crowned with tarsals
  and jutting scapulae
  elephant's toe-bones
      the shoulders of deified lovers
stone the colour of bone
  bleached and deadly
  under a noon sun or
  hissing in the soft rain
  drinking finite moisture
      from the bowl of sky
as the sea carves secret chambers
  echoes epitaphs, the hollow
  infinity of words
  the way a scream at night
  mingles with a dog's bark
      the hum of satellites

New moon, no moon
sky fathomless black
punctuated with gasps of stars,
gasps of lovers
warming to one another
under the chill breathless dome.

His hand moves, searches
for the warm moisture, milky way
swaying above him. She rides slowly,
calls out constellations with each breath.

He looks up, sees Venus,
reaches, but she is in orbit,
a slow rotating satellite
beaming down in a foreign language
out of reach   aurora
borealis beckons,
part of her follows, is lifted up
inverted and falling
into pin-pricks of light.

A meteor bursts and drops
past her left ear.
He sees the fine golden thread
Ariadne gave to Theseus
and he pulls her down
back to earth, makes her
forget stars
minotaurs.

Bird Watching

two point five seconds
the time it takes pigeons
to copulate
again, again
silhouetted on the roof
across the alley
beyond the words, the screen
the window
I look out of to avoid
eye strain but can't
help notice him
in the garden
behind the house
below the pigeons
the curve of his back
the hat he is wearing
a headdress for his clean-shaven
skull, the colour of milk
chocolate, calves and mouth
worthy of Rameses, shoulders too
broad and open to possibility.

Riding this high desert flood plain
beside a ridge of canyon snaking
along the river, the road
winding around imagined hills
spewing dust and the blush
of thistles in October sun
late afternoon edible autumn
raspberry, melon, tangerine
against a complement of green
lichen sunning on rock, silver
wormwood, sweet sage.

Across the road the desert becomes field
purple alfalfa, brilliant but stubborn
tight-lipped flowers
only some bees bother to pollinate.
So farmers import migrant bees
to pry open the reluctant buds,
a favourite feed for the rich cream of Jerseys
the marbled meat of Red Angus
the last meal of sad-eyed cattle
on their way to slaughter
as the ranchers file out
the auction over, the hamburgers gone
only straws of sperm
left for the breeders and all those
frustrated cows.

Not Narcissus

This is not who I am what
you want what I
said

not the blood red of
peonies in the late sun
flooding out onto a
perfect blue-
green lawn
not Kentucky
not a compliment

not the way salt
spills grain by grain onto the
stained table, the way
words are
day after day
after all is
not said

these stones
are not a crypt
do not have faces
of animals or birds
embedded in their rocky
jaws

this fireplace does not
burn wood, is not my
home, the voice
you hear
this face, your mirror
is definitely
not Narcissus

HER STRONG HANDS

For my mother's mother

After he died you went
west, left his memory
me   in the middle
of the bald prairie

for the wind to wash clean
for her strong hands to heal,
lift me out of your dark
grief, to mold, give me shape.

I watched her hands, knarled and quick
fold, mend, scrub
knead kneading dough
punching, pressing it out.

The swift snap of a chicken's
neck, bodies hopping and dancing
headless to the music of thunder
in an open field.

Her hands plucked out the feathers
until naked as new-borns she would
cut them up to boil
stack the jars high for winter.

The same hands that combed and
braided my hair could drown kittens
without hesitation. No thought
of their loss, the mother's swinging tits

no mouths to give the milk to.
I think of your heavy breasts
miles away,
all the milk in your body.

I had picked out an orange one
the runt, wanted to watch it grow, take shape
as I was growing, taking shape
but it was gone.

When I asked she said no room
no food, too many, it had to be.
Done, her eyes clear and deep
rare as bluebells along the gravel road.

Unnatural Acts

For my lost father

a residue of grief hangs in the trees
where a rope once swung
where they found her.

and before the crack of a shotgun
scattered his rage across the sand,
the wind, the waves warned me to leave
an act against nature
imminent.

a reckoning   a way out
of this strata of grey
a wasps' nest scraped
from minute layers of skin
the colour of dirt
     under nails.

you led me to them   leaving
as you did, in the dead
of winter, middle of night
your anguish smothered in rags and fumes,
your legacy a lacuna and shards of guilt
     a rupture in history   a hole
instead of arms
to fall into.

EUCALYPTUS

For my found father

Squeeze a bud of the Australian myrtaceous evergreen
between thumb and forefinger
and think of Vic's Vaporub, gently spread
on a little girl's bony chest
her croupy giggle,
my father's large hand.

Wild, medicinal
the most primitive of plants.
Cut stalks kept moist in a dark narrow vase
will grow for years
in their own fungus
sending diptych after diptych
of fan-shaped leaves searching
for light and meaning.

SHORT WAVE
For my grandfather

The voices came
from deep within the earth, resonant
with exotic language.
I watched you turn the phosphorescent dial
until scratchy moans congealed
into syllables hard as stones
crisp as prairie winters
soft and light as birds.

Mingled with theses voices,
your voice, strong and warm.
I would look up, see your words
drift down like seed propellers
out of sync, a galaxy away
your head too small for that huge body
the distortion of distance
a child's perspective.

Now your voice comes in gasps
or soft grating sounds
and you are only
half of yourself, cornered in
points of reference
gone.

The knot twisting in your spine
a wayward whorl
on an old elm, rooting in you
pulling you down

as you become smaller
your voice grows faint,
gathers static, draws you
into the earth, closer
to our other worlds.

STONE HOME

those stones
cool elliptical worlds
unto themselves
pure mass and weight
forcing definition
bullying imagination
into the picture
of table, chair
cold surface reality
against palm, legs, face

old bottles on the stone shelf
whisky brown
deep noxema royal, watery
depression glass

imagined lace curtains
cake baking in a stone oven
the thin grove of poplars, caragana
opening
to a bedroom, a man
home

simple, finite
respite from the infinite sky, sun
finger of wind
coaxing a small girl down a long gravel road.

EPITAPH

For Charlie

Now is beginning again
             now.
that he is gone

Forgetting his voice over
and over.   again
now that he is lost
in imagining.

Red shirt against blue sky
scent of vanilla
tawny brown burley
curling in wisps
of smoke. Fire and
water heavy with salt
tears wrapped in waves
and hitting the sand
                      over and over.

blackberries and honeybees
again

"Ba" Sking with Akhenaten and the Boys

In memory of Greg Curnoe

Today you are flying
as the hieroglyph for bird
implies the idea of bird
the ability to escape
the earth, the volatile spirit
mortality.

How many pharaohs' bones
have been crushed into tubes
of Egyptian Brown?

Today you will know.
You will meet them all.
Anubis, "opener of the way"
will introduce you,
the soul's tour-guide
      you can't miss him —
a skinny black dog with long ears,
he responds to the "h"
      in whistle,
to gestures in bas-relief.

Imagine the conversation you will have
sharing ancient secrets
learning the language
of stars and dead kings,
while someone prepares the obituary
chooses the casket
clears the debris of spokes and bent metal
off the road.

BAUDRILLARD ON THE BEACH

"I am the water that preserves your memory . . . "
— Jean Baudrillard, *Cool Memories II*

and laughs at this shore
this beach, only us
and two ducks
on it

or are we
is this
a place
where we wished to be
for so long now that we are here
we need a sign to tell us
a book
a map
is not the territory

the Aegean is so salty
you couldn't sink if you tried
I say, coaxing.
put it down, the word
simulacra is silly here
silly as ducks
on a sandy beach
all you need to do is slip
into this cool memory
lie back into the caress of waves
and taste it.

1st Relevation

I am soft sift / In an hourglass — at the wall . . .
— Gerard Manley Hopkins,
"The Wreck of the Deutshland"

I am soft sift
dip your fingers under my skin
like sand *in an hourglass* I melt
when you turn me under

palm your hands to
my mouth so I can lick the
calluses soft, but not before
I feel their sinew scrape thigh

at the wall, kneel
grasp the plank of my back
I am a see-saw, a boat, a
carpenter's plane. Rock me.

2ND RELEVATION

Kiss my hand to the dappled-with-damson west . . .
— Gerard Manley Hopkins,
"The Wreck of the Deutshland"

superfluid mirror of mercury
reflects a verdigris sky, clouds
dappled with damson
in its viscous skin

paddle churns a vortex of
longing, the lake licks my hand,
wavelets spread and ripple
from my fingers

remembering your touch
a spark of light ignites the sky,
above the rushes a strip
of tessellated rainbow hovers.

> *Warm-laid grave of a womb-life grey;*
> *Manger, maiden's knee;*
>
> — Gerard Manley Hopkins,
> "The Wreck of the Deutshland"

Consubstantial the alchemy
of body, blood   my cup
to your lips the consummate feast.
Gorged on flesh and falling
exhausted, into this *warm-laid grave*

limbo of desire, *womb-life*
grey and finally foreboding,
a plea for mercy, gentle
flagellation, remission of sin.

The Virgin is a myth, I say. Listen
to the timbre of trees whining in wind,
their longing for winter to strip them.

The heaven we ascend to in this musty manger,
your cheek *on the maiden's knee*
not imaginary or less than survival,
more than being
in place and time.

4TH RELEVATION

Father and fondler of heart thou has wrung:
Hast thy dark descending and most art merciful then.
— Gerard Manley Hopkins,
"The Wreck of the Deutshland"

Perhaps in a meadow when the moon
blooms full, bleeds light. When whispering
grasses and ghosts beckon. *Father, fondler*
of my heart will you come, tell me where
in the universe your atoms are scattered.

Perhaps steal away without notice, you thought
so quiet a leaving, the last heave of breath.
In the *dark descending* did you ever glance back,
wonder where your traces would linger
what patterns your shadow makes on my soul.

Perhaps a merciful art of departure. A weaning
and wend, the way up, to light. Bliss intermittent
when the heart opens. A loon call of longing
wrung from my throat, discovering your name,
your face, your voice in me.

ERRANT REVERIES

INTERFERENCE WITH THE HYDRANGEA

For David Donnell

Sitting in the outdoor patio of a Harbord street cafe
under a spreading oak and baroque music playing at a
tasteful decibel, listening to the couple next to me
discuss the logistics of deck gardening and the strategic
placement of hydrangeas versus creeping thyme,
deck gardens being the latest rage among the upwardly
mobile and the literary set, what with poets writing
books on the subject and probably making lots of
money on them or at least more money than on their
poetry. In fact this week's gardening article in the *Globe*
is all about rhododendrons and how they like shade
and how in 1656, John Tradescant went to places like
China and the Himalayas to get them. And I think
about how I wouldn't hear this conversation in
Moose Jaw or Red Deer and also think how much better
the chilled cucumber soup would taste with a few
delicately chopped sprigs of cilantro instead of boring
parsley. The ice tea is caffeine-free mint, real mint leaves
not the dried tea bag kind and they use raw sugar or
honey only and don't give you any butter with the whole
grain bread even if you ask for it. So here I sit reading
China Blues, enjoying the sun sneaking past the leaves and
summer breeze in spite of myself and this incorrect
craving for red meat.

The middle of a busy Saturday on the Drive and cars lined up in a row slowly pulling forward at the green, then faster and clearly, there they were driving through the intersection, looking deep into each other's eyes and gesturing wildly with both hands as their blue Buick sped forth and nearly missed a woman with a cane taking too much time to cross the road although the light had just turned and they should have been watching because the woman couldn't watch, or yell, although they wouldn't have heard anyway, being deaf and busy trying to talk.

OK so I said deaf, not hearing impaired because it is a nice word and we should use it because it says what it means and the soft blowing sound of the *f* like the rush of air from a hand moving through space and forming a word without sound like watching TV with the noise turned off. Mute, deaf, dumb, blind, lame, crippled, retarded, depressed, suicidal. Words that say what the thing is not what it's not. Words that don't waste time or breath. Not correct but not wrong. Words that pack a wallop. Words for the strong of heart, not the emotionally impaired.

THE QUESTION OF THE OBSERVER

Experience is not reality, but that which we distinguish.
— Umberto Maturana

The most common mammal in the mountains, the Columbian ground squirrel rarely plays in traffic. This is yet another gambit for survival, alongside learning to elude predators.

There it sat, on its haunches, paws tucked up against its rust-coloured chest rising and falling to rapid rhythmical heartbeats. Contemplating that the structure of the nervous system changes with living. Tiny ears flat against its head. Unblinking, it watched me watch it. Clearly aware that this structural change is contingent on the history of its interactions.

The ground squirrel invited me into its burrow, but of course I declined, not wanting to set a dangerous precedent and being aware of this delicate dance of nature, two beings intertwined in reciprocal structural coupling. The observer observing the observed observing the observer. Although I would have liked to have seen its home, the intricate maze of tunnels and escape burrows. And I was curious, so I asked. In the spring, upon awakening from your deep hibernation, why don't you follow the familiar corridors already laboriously dug? Why do you burrow straight up? A yearning for sky? An impatience to begin anew?

He tilted his furry head slightly downward, eyes raised in bemusement at my notion of his reality. The world is not what we observe, but what we do, he said flicking his tail and ducking back into his burrow.

VIPER BATS, A TRUE TALE

For Clint

Yep, watch out for them viper bats,
sneaky critters, they climb up your pant leg
blinded by daylight, think it is a hairy-
barked tree. Drawn to the warmth they
nestle their small claws into your soft
flesh. Thinking only of the climb, the
juncture, there, crotch branching out
chalice-like to cradle and curl up in.
Look up, look way up. They are only
poisonous if rabid and pubic hair isn't
long enough for them to get
tangled up in anyhow.

Tools R Us

For Loren Teed

It's not everyday I have lunch at the Co-Op
looking out over the display of fridges and stoves.
The borsch was good. Real sour cream and sweet
memories of my wild youth. 72 beer in the trunk of
a Cortina. Three girls and a homemade tent. Now
the trunk packed with serious tools. Paints, canvass,
books, computer. But absent brushes and printer
driver so I guess we need to regress a bit, think
about what we would do with a stick, some leafy
branches, a bare patch of dirt. Ponder hand prints in
mud, the pattern of bodies pressed into the grass.
After all, in the whole scheme of things, these marks
we make are only scratchings on the shell of history
for some small child to come along and bury with
her other toys.

Funny, today I looked at that tree cracked open in the
forest a sad stump once a giant among spruce.
Yesterday I would have seen firewood but today
something about the light the wind shoving clouds
about, flicking sunlight here and there, perhaps the
moan of sapless branches, or perhaps just morning
after not enough sleep and the thoughts not turning
off without the turquoise pills beside my bed just in
case except almost always now as I nod off the thoughts
racing what if she doesn't feed my cats or the cheque
doesn't clear or they reject my poems or there isn't
enough work or he really is a psychopath or the nastur-
tiums die due to lack of worry.

red dog on grey concrete running a fine line along the
narrow strip of stone that separates his old bones, wet
fur from tonnes of metal whizzing past his one clear eye,
the other black and matted closed. but tail up, striding
along as if to say i'm ok, not lost, just running, running
along this freeway bridge for the hell of it because i'm a
dog without a leash, not without a home no don't think
that don't call the pound, an old dog like me wouldn't
last a week in that place. rather walk this thin grey line
than become one, a slow finger of smoke curling up to
a low grey sky.

DAILY NEWS JULY 4, 1998

And Canada has played major
in probing the red planet. Possibly the
first man on Mars a Canadian. Why not?
We have a sense of humour, wear
practical shoes. Are concerned about orphans
and widows and don't leave our participles
dangling. Out there, silent vacuous space inhales
light and time. Somewhere an asteroid snuck in
between orbits of earth and the sun to its back.
Its silent collision course perfectly invisible,
until today. Some bright scientist caught
a glimpse. DK36 nothing to worry about. It's
the ones we haven't found yet can hit us when
we least expect it, like the guy from Tampa
knocked out by a stripper's breasts. Suing
for whiplash. And they say volcanoes
on the moon of Jupiter, not Diamond Dolls,
may be the hottest place in the solar system. Try a
highway out of Florida. Burning wall of bush and
stranded motorists trying to run, run out of gas
as they idle on melting asphalt. Hell on wheels.
And drought down under has Australian farmers
opting out. Not as many as South Korea where
they put on a shirt and tie each morning, pretend
to still have a job. After awhile, jumping
is better than lying. And in the north,
they just starve by the millions.

texture of woven cotton harsh rubbing against up
against thighs the smell of smoke and crushed twigs
of poplar, sap running running out a raging river
churning you up pushing under, spewing forth words
like promises and not quite letting you up for air in the
broken daylight.

texture of raw Bedouin weaving rasping scapula and hip
and knees — up, up high reaching to stars like sequins
on Elvis's jacket.

take me to the movies aunt Bernice. only four
and already craving the image of heroic sex. you ain't
nothing but a monkey climbing tree posture. there's
the rub. the texture of hair twining against. bristles
like a grandfather's whiskers only not on cheek.

The sky over Kutna Hora is smoky blue like the lilacs
outside the cathedral its buttresses flying high to meet
it. Sun through the stained glass spiking a medieval
painting of Christ and his disciples talking or whatever
his hand up in that comforting gesture that means it's
OK your sins are purged if you follow this path, the one
snaking along through the dark wood overgrown with
brambles.

Kde ye toilettee? Kde ye autobus? Kde ye salvation?

And the only other person sitting on the only shaded
bench in the square can't answer me, my language too
foreign, the thought of salvation too absurd after
seventy years in a country of metamorphosis, black
jokes and bloody Spring. The others had long gone
I was sure and the heat bouncing off the white walls
of the open square. Alone, in this town or one like it
where my grandfather had smoked his pipe, ate soup
from mushrooms picked in the field, played chess and
drank fine Pilsner. In this country he and his brothers
escaped. Not one of his seeds his blood left behind to
germinate. A genealogy barren as minefields as
Terrezine where wild flowers and lots of lilacs grow and
weave their heady scent around the bunkers now.
Perhaps a hint of caramel in the skin, or eyes glowing
too fiercely, or for breaking out into spontaneous song.
Now gone. Only one old woman, Placatkova, the wife
of, left. Glad to be kept hidden in the hazy present
where she is safe to forget.

Kde ye autobus po Praha? I ask the old man sitting next to me on the one bench in the shade of the square in the middle of that ancient town once rich with silver that King Charles used to build his Camelot, right here in the middle of Bohemia or is it Moravia, with. It is getting late and I don't know this place, this language, no one left to look for and I want to go home or at least someplace familiar. Perhaps he recognizes a glint of history or fear. *Napravo* he points, writes down a time. Over there. To the right. *Dêkuji,* I smile into his smoky blue eyes like the sky only looking up instead of pressing down.

CatoptRomancer

*"Subterranean water in motion
has by its field of force,
which is continually active,
a very real effect on every human organism.
No human being can sleep with impunity
for many nights continuously
above a subterranean stream."*

— Henri Mager,
"Water Diviners and Their Methods"

1 INCANTATION

You must take a mirror, preferably round
in which you look at yourself
daily for a year,

place it in a vessel of water
preferably glass and
also preferably round,

then place three stones
in the water
around the mirror

one yellow, one green, one white
and at midnight,
when the moon is new or full

and by the light
of two candles only
gaze into the mirror

in the water in the vessel
of glass, and tell me
what you see.

2   Wind

I hold the image of you
in the palm of my hand
my mind's   I
a small girl, alone
in the middle of the parched field
I can feel the hot wind
on your bare arms
baking your rare pale flesh
a crimson umber
in the oven of summer.

Endless blue horizon sky pulls you backward squinting
against the brilliance
against the heat
against the pushing bully
wind.

Incessant male probing howling wind
pulling hair
lifting skirts
hurling dust
into eyes, mouth, ears
any crevice or orifice.

The table is set for dinner,
covered with a thin cloth
to keep the wind's gritty sediment
from filming plates
greying the sugar.

Her jaw set in a rigid line.
You learned it is best to be silent
when she looks like this,
nerves raw from the constant
wind rattling windows
against parched sills,
the wood bleached grey
by months, years of cloudless, rainless days.

Dust collects between glass and waxpaper
inching opaquely
upward.

They said she was the Tsar's niece
escaped   with a lover
to this splayed out land
its open-armed promise
of freedom.

He watched her go
into a field   grasp handfuls of wheat
wrench it up by the roots
the smell of torn stalk and earth,
her own sweat
as she pulls and pulls
as the wind pushes
the fine cloth into the curves of her body
until the straw slits into her
pale hands, now swollen crimson
the hands of a peasant.

My first image of a witch
this angry young woman
now bent and weathered
as the cane she flails at cars, people, roads
everything that separates her
from the river, the prairie
miles of sky blue as his eyes
fields yellow as his hair,
this land that worked him
into the ground, the bleak
expanding void of it
without him.

Grandmother's threats
"if you don't eat your supper
I'll put you in the oven."

Imagining scorched black flesh, our hair
the smell of burnt feathers,
and the sound of her laughter
at the look on our faces.
A witch's laugh.

Desire for beauty
Power over men
Fear of beauty
Power over women
Fear of youth
Power over age
Desire for wisdom
Power over youth
Desire for/fear of
women
Desire for/fear of
men
Desire for
Fear of
Power over

5 Divination

Her hands reveal rivers of veins
under petal-thin skin, the rush
of blood almost visible
as long skeletal fingers
clutch the arms of the branch
its fork proclaiming water
angels, rain.

Others use whalebone or metal.
She says the wand doesn't matter
as much as feeling the pulse of it,
its life or death. And then she begins
steely eyes burrow to currents
of blood, marrow of bone.

> *A body is mostly water*
> *she'd say*
> *with a little food*
> *colouring.*

They watch her balance their future
on the tip of the wand as it leads her
             forward and around
an invisible partner in a silent dance,
it begins to vibrate and swing
pulling her closer.

*"In the summer, the children drove a pony to school
but in the winter, the pony was too slow,
the highway too heavy, and the ride too cold, so they walked.
It was four miles and they walked on the railway tracks
as they could make better time there than on the road."*

— Les Rowley, *Rural Roots*, 1987

The first winter in years with enough
snow, they forgot how to act
in a blizzard.

The boy only five,
ice pellets stinging his face
hard to run or breathe
the wind scattering his screams
like dandelion seeds
the snow heavier and heavier
up to his knees, impossible to see
the barn only yards from the house
cinnamon buns in the warm oven
and his legs fold under him
like a cut-out valentine
he thinks of his sister
      and falls
into the soft cool whiteness.

She doesn't use the rod this time.
Her grey eyes track the waist-high drifts
and settle like a snowflake on
two blue fingers
pointing to heaven.

and the wind continues
and the wind continues
and the wind continues
and the wind continues
and the wind continues
and the wind continues
and the wind continues

What was the bridegroom's name?	*Sweet William*
What was the bride's name?	*Rose*
What did she wear on her head?	*Orange blossom*
What did she wear on her feet?	*Lady's slippers*
What colour was her dress?	*Pink*
What colour were her eyes?	*Violet*
With what did her husband govern her?	*Golden Rod*
Her parting words to her friends?	*Forget-me-not*
Her farewell gift to her father?	*Bleeding Heart*
What heavenly bodies lighted their way?	*Sunflowers*
How enduring was their love?	*Everlasting*

8 EARTH

Her hands comb the soil
crumble clumps of earth
finger iridescent patina
of frost on leaves
under the moon's thin

insignificant arc
she walks out and out
into the dark field
feels the power of being
invisible, of no one knowing

where   oh where
she begins to dance and sing
inhales the fragrance of hay
the breath of night
longs to be swept away

from his grunting gnawing rawness
this dirt this field this prairie
stretching on forever and ever
without hope
amen.

The next morning he brings her the almanac
pours her coffee.

> *September, 1944 ninth month*
> *moon in Capricorn*
> *clear and pleasant up to the 27th*
> *then threatening skies and winds*
> *foretell storms.*

He has opened it to page 24
a testimonial of splendid results,
a message
for women only.
She takes a sip of coffee

> *Only women know the real meaning*
> *of the "troublesome time."*

picks up the teaspoon

> *Only women can appreciate*
> *the real difficulties*
> *that these recurring days bring.*

drags the sugarbowl across the table

> *At this time the organs of the pelvic region*
> *are congested and easily irritated.*

scoops out two heaping teaspoons
one after the other
tilts the spoon slowly,
granules cascading a crystal waterfall
into her cup.

> *An excellent medicine for this purpose is*
> *Dr. Morse's Indian Root Pills.*

She lifts the cup to her lips
purses them and sucks
the coffee in
with a long, slurping draw.

> *The pills are made from vegetable ingredients*
> *and act promptly and thoroughly.*

She can feel him watching but doesn't look up.

> *Used as directed they should not*
> *gripe or nauseate.*

She picks up the spoon and pulls
the sugar toward her,

> *Buy a package today in case you need them.*

bends her head over the bowl
grasps the spoon like a shovel
and begins to dig,
sugar spilling out of her mouth
like foam.

> *Dr. Morse's Indian Root Pills . . .*

He grasps her hair, the force
of his hand spewing a blizzard of sugar
across the room.

> *They make you feel brighter.*

The last words she remembers reading.

Just past Forget, Saskatchewan,
not a house in sight
only a sign, a shrine
where sometime, years ago
the Virgin appeared.

The two-lane black top
stretches ahead, defines infinity
as the horizon's curve
pulls peripheral vision into a tight band
around the skull.

The sky heavy with thunderheads
the weight of cobalt
pressing down on a field of rape
its screaming yellow
its pungent perfume

> the bottle of *Ben Hur*
> I gave you for mother's day
> *worse than Evening in Paris*
> your barbed words
> blew to where I listened,
> a thistle on wire
> and the space between us
> widening

like the prairie, the unforgiving sun
bleaching flesh of wheat
bones of snow
eyes never wide open
against the wide open sky.

11 Wishing

Frigid fists of wind
beat against face
forehead throbs, eyes ache
hair stiff with frozen breath, tears
as feet track a line across an infinite field
of squeaking snow
40 below and nothing
but stars are out.

She is twelve-years-old
walking to the edge
the seam
where snow meets stars
to fall
into cool, numb
dreamless
sleep.

If carragana pods are plumper than usual.
If a fox's fur thickens early.
If birds fly south too soon.

If leaves turn unexpectedly.
If branches of mountain ash
are weighted with berries.

If a handful of wheat thrown into the air
always falls to the south,
pushed by wind from the north.

If rain and frost come
before harvest, pushed
by wind from the north.

If a horse goes mad
from the constant push and howl
of wind from the north.

If a December baby
arrives stillborn, the echo if its cry
only the north wind pushing.

Confessions

Epigraphs are from *The Confessions of St. Augustine*. Poems 1 to 4 use the 1983 translation by E. M. Blaiklock. Poems 5 to 10 use the Edward Bouverie Pusey translation (1800-1882).

In the 7th Confession, the word "discandy" is from Shakespeare, who used it only twice — both times in *Antony and Cleopatra*. It means to melt, to fragment, to disolve. *The Arden Shakespeare*, ed. M.R. Ridley (Routledge, 1954).

Relevations

The definition of "radiant energy" is from the *Oxford Dictionary of Physics*, 1985.

The epigraph for "Beaudrillard on the Beach" is from *Cool Memories II*, trans. Chris Turner (Polity Press, 1992).

Epigraphs for the 1st to 4th Relevation are from Gerard Manley Hopkins's "The Wreck of the Deutshland." *Gerard Manley Hopkins: Poems and Prose*, ed. W.H. Gardner (Penguin, 1963).

Errant Reveries

The epigraph for "The Question of the Observer" is from a lecture by Chilean biologist and enactivist Umberto Maturana on "The Biology of Human Relationships" (Simon Fraser University, 1992).

CatoptRomancer

Catoptromancy: Divination by looking into a mirror placed in a vessel of water. (*Concise Oxford Dictionary*)

"A Floral Wedding," author unknown. Found notes in a 1928 edition of *The Boston Cooking School Cookbook* by Fannie Farmer.

Mager, Henri, "Water Diviners and Their Methods"; translated from the fourth edition of *Les sourciers et leurs procédés* by A. H. Bell. London, G. Bell and Sons Ltd., 1931.

Rowley, Les. Excerpt from *Rural Roots*, published by the Brada, Easthill, Roecliffe Historical Society, 1987.

Dr. Morse's *Indian Root Pills Almanac*, an advertising flyer published by the W.H. Comstock Company, Limited, Brockville, Ont., 1944.

Acknowledgements

Some of these poems have previously been published in *Hub City, Tongue Tied, subTerrain,* and *The Temple.* An earlier version of *CatoptRomancer* was published as a chapbook by Relevations Publications. Earlier versions of Confessions 1 to 4 appeared in the anthology *Listening with the Ear of the Heart: Writers at St. Peter's.* (St. Peter's College Press, 2003).

Thanks to the Ontario Arts Council Writer's Reserve Program and the following publishers for supporting my work: Rampike, Aya/Mercury Press, *Open Letter, Books in Canada, Fireweed, The Idler,* and Cormorant Books.

Special thanks to The Saskatchewan Writers Guild, Emma Lake and St. Peter's Writers/Artists Colonies, and the Banff Centre Writing Studio for providing a place and time to write.

My heartfelt gratitude goes to those who have helped with the shaping and honing of this manuscript — particulary Susan Musgrave for her keen eye and gracious ear. Also to Don McKay and Helen Humphrys for their insightful and generous critique, and everyone at the 2003 Banff Studio who helped me through the editing process.

Love and thanks to Robert McNealy, Paul Dutton, Betsy Rosenwald, Charles Potts, Kate Van Dusen, Victor Coleman, Sue Nevill, David Lee, Rod MacIntyre, Steven Smith, Fiona Lam, Bill Klebeck, Kathleen Whelan, Dave Margoshes, Rhona McAdam, Hilary Clark, and Betsy Warland for their support and encouragement.